CONTENTS

GYMNASTICS FOR KIDS AGES 3~7

Dancy Kelsey Noble

LEISURE PRESS New York

A publication of Leisure Press.
597 Fifth Avenue, New York, N.Y. 10017
Copyright © 1983 by Leisure Press
All rights reserved. Printed in the U.S.A.

ISBN 0-918438-86-1
Library of Congress Number: 81-83013

Front cover photo: Cheryl Traendly
Back cover artwork: Joe Litow
Cover design: Diana Goodin

PART I
BEFORE
WE START

1
WHY TEACH THE YOUNG ONES?

In the past, young bodies developed naturally through locomotor skills such as walking, throwing, jumping, running, hopping, skipping, and galloping. They were also developed through such skills as climbing, lifting, and general play. It has become apparent that during the 60's and 70's children lacked developmental opportunities and the creativity that goes along with them. Television as a "spectator sport" has become a substitute for participation in exercise among young children. Thus, by the time these children are of preschool and kindergarten age, they have not developed their muscle groups adequately towards better flexibility, strength, and agility. They have become deficient in those basic physiological functions that are vital to mastering a multitude of concepts enabling them to live better lives.

Experience is the best teacher. A child below the age of five can absorb and retain large amounts of information at a remarkable rate and has amazing amounts of energy with which to pursue his inquisitiveness,

7

plus a monumental desire to learn. Therefore, gymnastic skills can be learned and absorbed at an early age and some of the same skills at the Tiny Tots levels may be taught at the preschool level. Actually, skill development at this early age proves that learning at five is easier than at six, and learning at four is easier than at five.

Five levels of progression are outlined in this book. The first two levels are for Preschoolers, ages three and four, with emphasis on gymnastic-like activities including warm-ups and stunts. The next three levels are designed for the Tiny Tots, ages five, six and seven, and offer selected gymnastic activities, warm-ups and stunts. These levels permit each child to advance at his or her own pace. Even if a child is not yet five years old, but completes the requirements of both preschool levels, he or she can advance to the Tiny Tots level.

There are many benefits to be derived from early participation in gymnastic activities. Just a few of them are:

- Learning to follow directions.
- Developing listening skills.
- Improving peer group relationships.
- Increasing self-esteem as well as self-confidence.
- Developing visual perception through locomotor movements in warm-ups and through the trampoline and balance beam activities.
- Improving hand-eye coordination through the use of hoops, balloons, wands, balls, ropes and bar activities.
- Creating total body coordination through body positions and movements in using both sides of the body equally.
- Learning to transfer weight and apply force, as well as support one's own weight and maintain balance.
- Becoming aware of the body parts and the body's position in space.
- Developing flexibility through stretching exercises.
- Increasing strength with the use of the apparatus.
- Improving normal neuromuscular development (involving large and small muscles) through a planned program.
- Preparing the child for reading readiness by expanding his/her speaking and hearing vocabulary. This may be controversial but I am convinced that early motor perceptual activity geared to physical experience helps to prepare children for learning to read.

And last, but by far not least, it is hoped that this book will encourage parents to become involved with the teaching of gymnastics to their young children. Parent involvement promotes awareness of their child's strengths and weaknesses. It in fact becomes a learning experience for the parent as well as the child. The parent's role should be that of constant encouragement, never criticism. Parents and children must approach the mastery of gymnastic activities as a fun, creative and exciting event. With the influence of past Olympics, more and more people are becoming aware of the importance of being physically active. Who knows? Perhaps under the moptop of your three-year-old may lurk the gymnastic talents of a Nadia Comeneci or an Olga Korbut.

It is to be hoped that experiencing these activities and warm-ups will teach the children to develop good habits in keeping their bodies fit for a lifetime of participation in a variety of physical activities.

2
SAFETY AWARENESS

What is gymnastic safety? Simply listing rules and regulations is not a sufficient answer to that question. The preparation of a safe environment is a great responsibility. It is up to the person in charge to see to it that *everyone* involved with the teaching of gymnasts, including the various coaches *and* parents, are aware of the duties and responsibilities of preparing a safe environment. They, in turn, must instill this need for safety precautions in the gymnasts themselves.

Listed below are some preventive measures. But no list is exhaustive; each coach, parent, and even child involved in gymnastics is urged and encouraged to add to this list constantly.

- Proper warm-ups before each activity or session begins.
- See to it that each child takes the readiness test given in Chapter 5 which will reveal his/her individual weaknesses and strengths.
- The slow, step-by-step progression in teaching gymnastic skills is a most important factor leading to success and safety.
- Children should wear proper attire; a leotard for the girls, shorts and T-shirts for either boys and girls, and of course a warm-up suit for both.
- Nylon socks are very dangerous on varnished floors or the balance beam; therefore, terry footlets, cotton socks, or just plain bare feet are recommended.
- The girls should not wear jewelry and, if their hair is long, it should not be unbound. None of the children should chew gum.

- While mats are not the complete answer to eliminating or reducing injuries, there are some factors to be kept in mind:
  a. The gymnastic activities to be performed.
  b. The ages and fitness of the child or children.
  c. The nature of the equipment or apparatus to be used. Obviously, if the child is going to jump from a piece of equipment, more mats are needed. Just plain commonsense needs to be exercised in determining the size and number of mats needed for a particular activity.
  d. The condition of the mats—are they old and worn?
  e. Although absolute requirements cannot be set for every situation, the differences between resiliency and shock absorbency of the mats should be understood.
  f. Mats should never be unused. There is always a place for additional ones.
  g. Always remember, mats are not fail-safe. Nothing can substitute for proper step-by-step progression in instruction, spotting, making sure the child is listening, and again, just plain commonsense in the teaching of gymnastics.
- To prevent hands from slipping off the equipment such as bars, rings, and ropes, it is highly recommended that chalk of magnesium carbonate be used before attempting these activities. This chalk can be found at the drugstore.

Although spotting is mentioned briefly above, it merits more concern. Spotting is the technique of observing and assisting the gymnast in order to make learning of skills easier and to minimize the risks of mistakes. Hand spotting is spotting with the hands alone and is wisely used at beginning levels. In hand spotting, the instructor (and/or parent) will assist the child, staying close to him/her and even be in contact most of the time. The goal in protective spotting is to control the action. When the child is first learning a new skill, contact should be made even if it seems to be unnecessary. Here are some other spotting safety tips:

Although spotting is mentioned briefly above, it merits more concern. Spotting is the technique of observing and assisting the gymnast in order to make learning of skills easier and to minimize the risks of mistakes. Hand spotting is spotting with the hands alone and is wisely used at beginning levels. In hand spotting, the instructor (and/or parent) will assist the child, staying close to him/her and even be in contact most of the time. The goal in protective spotting is to control the action. When the child is first learning a new skill, contact should be made even if it seems to be unnecessary. Here are some other spotting safety tips:

- Be constantly alert, anticipating a fall or an incorrect movement.
- Watch for an early or late release from a dismount off the rings and bars.
- Follow the child all the way through the skill, including the landing.
- Do not hesitate to overspot, especially during the early stages of learning a skill.
- Whenever there is a reasonable doubt about an unsafe situation, take immediate action.
- The observant spotter should watch the child's head, which is the key to the control of the movement.
- The spotter must know where to stand to be most effective. This will vary according to the apparatus and the skill being performed. In general, the spotter should position himself between the performer and the place on the floor where the child is most likely to land. Many spotters stand too far away; thus, when the child falls, the spotter cannot move in fast enough to break the fall. However, the spotter should not stand so close that he could hamper the gymnast or expose himself to injury or a collision. Another reason for standing close is leverage.

The trampoline is a favorite of children but it can be dangerous. Some special safety tips for the trampoline are:

- There must be a minimum of *four* spotters standing around the trampoline (not sitting on the apparatus) when it is in use.
- No somersaults should be allowed. An exception may be made when belt spotting, and two spotters should be next to the gymnast, one on each side.
- The trampoline should be kept locked when not in use.
- Policies for emergency care should be preplanned.
- Overhead clearance above a trampoline should be adequate for safe use, according to the skills being taught or practiced.
- There should be no obstructions beneath the trampoline.

Most of the safety tips given in this chapter were taken from the Official Manual of the United States Gymnastic Safety Association, Eugene Wettstone, editor.

PART II
PRESCHOOL
CHILDREN
Ages 3 & 4

3
WARM-UP EXERCISES

Performing warm-ups to music is not only great fun but beneficial to everyone's body. Warm-ups increase the heart rate and produce an increased flow of blood so that oxygen is delivered faster to all the cells of the body, thus raising the general fitness level and permitting better performance. If the child's muscles are cold when he attempts a cartwheel, he could strain a muscle. A child who is warmed up, whose muscles are in readiness before he performs will be less prone to injury. For very young children, ten to fifteen minutes of warm-up is required.

The first eight exercises deal with getting the body warmed up as well a strengthening the legs. Exercises nine through sixteen deal with stretching and strengthening the body. Total time involved is ten to fifteen minutes. All exercises are done to music to add a little more fun.

- **Walking:** With good posture and swinging arms, walk around a large circle several times.
- **Jogging:** Slow jog, moving elbows back and forth and circling legs as in riding a bicycle. After several times around the circle, reverse and jog the other way around the circle.

- **Running:** At a faster pace, run counter-clockwise around the circle several times and then clockwise several times.
- **Side gallop:** This is a step-together-step, leading with the right foot, (right, left, right) gallop around the circle several times. Repeat to the left leading with the left foot.
- **Jumping:** With both feet together, jump five times forward, stop, jump five times backwards. Repeat this three times.
- **Hopping:** With one foot at a time, hop five times forward on the right, stop, hop five times backwards. Repeat on the left foot. Repeat this three times.
- **Jog backwards:** Jog counter-clockwise several times around the circle, then clockwise several times.
- **Ankle exercises:** Walk high on the balls of the feet around the circle, then change to walking on the heels around the circle. Roll ankles to the outside and walk on the outside of the feet around the circle. Then roll ankles to the inside so the knees are turned in and walk on the inside of the feet around the circle. Repeat the whole sequence three times.

Warm-up Exercises

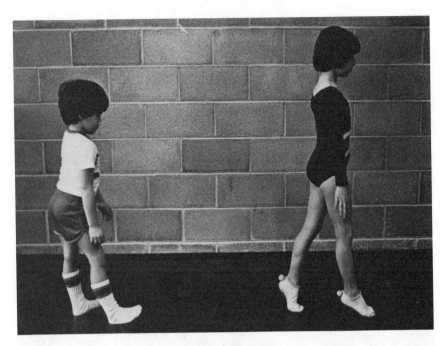

Ankle exercises.

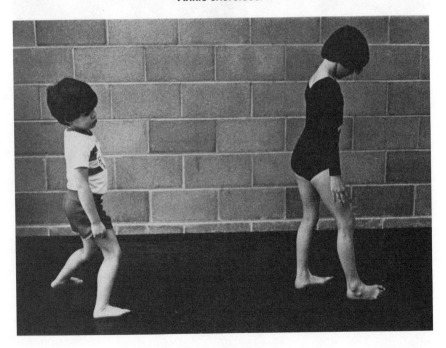

STRETCHING EXERCISES

All stretching exercises should be performed slowly and smoothly without bouncing. After repeating three or four times, the individual should begin to feel the muscles stretching out and loosening up. Hold each stretched position for three to five seconds, and then return to the starting position.

Side stretches.

- **Side stretches:** Standing with legs apart and arms overhead, lean to the right and the left, going as far as the body can stretch. Stretch forward with a flat back to finish the stretches. Repeat three times.
- **Side stretches on the floor:** Sitting on the floor, legs stretched out with toes pointed, stretch arms overhead for a starting position. Lean to the right, touching toes with nose to knee; hold. Stretch up and lean to the left; hold. Stretch up and lean forward; hold. Repeat three times.
- **Back of the legs stretch:** In a squat position with hands on the floor, raise the buttocks up to a stretched leg position, pushing the knees back; hold; return to a squat. Repeat three times.
- **Bridges:** Lying on back, hands flat on the floor with thumbs next to the ears, knees bent, and the feet flat on the floor. Push body up with arms to a straight arm extension, with the feet still flat on the floor. Start with two bridges and increase to five. The child must be supported at the upper back to allow for a full arm stretch. At the beginning, children like to push with their legs and toes and remain on their head, but the

Side stretches on the floor.

Back of the legs stretch.

Warm-up Exercises

Bridges.

Rocker.

Roll up—roll back.

Straight body push-up position.

Sit-ups.

purpose of this exercise is to stretch as well as strengthen the upper back and the arms.

- **Rocker:** Lying face down on the stomach, knees bent, grab ankles and rock forward and backward. This stretches the chest, arms, and the front of the legs.
- **Roll up - roll back:** From a sitting position, hug knees and roll back onto shoulders, hips being higher than the shoulders, and without stopping, roll up to a sitting position. Do this several times to stretch the back after the tightening of the muscles resulting from exercise #12 and #13. This also is the end part of the forward roll.

STRENGTHENING EXERCISES

- **Straight body push-up position:** Hold this position for ten seconds and then jump back to a squat position; then back out to a push-up position and hold for ten seconds. Repeat one more time. Make sure the back is flat and not arched with the tummy pulled in.
- **Sit-ups:** Feet are held by a parent or friend in a bent-knee position, with hands behind the head or stretched overhead. Lift the head and shoulders toward the knees and roll back down *very slowly* to the starting position.

24

4
GYMNASTIC-LIKE ACTIVITIES FOR PRESCHOOLERS

These gymnastic-like activities are based on a level of progression, so that the child can advance at his or her own pace safely. Most of the skills are lead-up skills that pertain to gymnastic skills.

Start with Level I on each activity and complete the level before going on to Level II. For example, the child should do all the activities on the balance beam of Level I before going on to Level II of the balance beam.

At the end of sections on Preschooler and Tiny Tot activities, there is a check-off list for each activity level. Thus there is no question of what the child has achieved and what to do next on that activity, or what the child is still trying to achieve.

LEVEL I

HANGING ROPES
(use chalk on hands)

- Jump and hold the body in a bent-arm position for three to five seconds.

- Pull the body up to a stand from a sitting position, moving the hands up the rope, hand-over-hand; come back down hand-under-hand to the sitting position. The feet are held in a fixed position for easier climb.

Hanging ropes.

BALANCE BEAM

The beam is six inches high from the floor, with two to three-inch padding under the beam. The length of the beam (if home-made) can be up to 16 feet in length and the width can be from 4 to 6 inches. Make sure it is level and steady. It could be padded with indoor-outdoor carpet stretched and glued around the whole beam.

* With eyes focused on the end of the beam, walk forward to the end and then walk backward. Repeat for five minutes. Place hands on the shoulders for better balance.
* Walk sidewards the length of the beam with eyes focused forward and hands on shoulders.
* Dog walk: On all fours, feet and hands, walk to the end of the beam. Most of the weight should be forward.

Balance beam—walking forward.

Walking sidewards the length of the beam.

Dog walk.

SINGLE BAR
(use chalk for hands)

- Chin-ups: Lead up to this by asking the child to put his chin on the bar and let his body come down slowly to a straight arm hang (chin-downs). Fingers are wrapped around the bar facing the child.
- Pull-ups: Lead up to this by requesting the child to put his chin on the bar and let his or her body come down slowly to a straight-arm hang (pull-downs). Fingers are wrapped around the bar away from the child.
- Work on one good chin-up and one good pull-up from a straight body hang.
- Swing side to side, traveling across the bar, sliding hands as the child swings.

Chin-ups.

Pull-ups.

Swinging side to side.

TRAMPOLINE

All skills are executed in the center of the trampoline, with four spotters standing around the trampoline. The children learn to jump at low levels, medium levels, and at a high level, according to which skill they are attempting.

• To help the child develop coordination of arms and legs for jumping on the trampoline, stand behind him and show him how to bring his arms forward, up overhead, and around in front as he jumps. In other words, as the arms go up, the body goes up, and as the arms come down, the body comes down.

Helping the child develop coordination of arms and legs.

Jumping.

Stopping with knees bent.

Bouncing on the knees.

Dog bounce.

Dog drop.

- Jump three times and then stop with knees bent, so as to lower the body for more control.
- Bounce on the knees with the body straight from the knees to the shoulders, and circle the arms around to make the body bounce to a stand.
- Dog bounce: On knees and hands, bounce on the trampoline until the knees and hands are bouncing at the same time off the trampoline. Then come up to a stand from the dog bounce. This takes a little practice, as the knees want to bounce but the hands do not want to push off. Once coordinated, it is easy.
- From a stand, drop down on all fours to the dog bounce position, and return to a stand. This is called a dog drop.

SAMPLE CHECK-OFF LIST OR CARDS FOR PRESCHOOLERS AT LEVEL I

Name _____

LEVEL I

Hanging Ropes
____ • Jump and hold 3-5 seconds
____ • Pull body to stand from sitting

Balance Beam
____ • Walks: forward and backwards
____ • Walk sidewards
____ • Dog walk

Single Bar
____ • Chin-ups; chin-downs
____ • Pull-ups; pull-downs
____ • One good pull-up and one good chin-up
____ • Swing side to side across bar

Trampoline
____ • Learning to jump
____ • Stopping for control
____ • Bounce on knees
____ • Dog bounce
____ • Dog drop to stand

Stunts
____ • Elephant walk
____ • Duck walk
____ • Three-legged walk
____ • Dog walk
____ • Shoulder rest
____ • Bridge
____ • Log roll
____ • Crab walks
____ • Rabbit hop
____ • Kangaroo

LEVEL II

HANGING ROPES
(use chalk on hands)

- Pull body up to a stand from a lying position, hand over hand; come back down, hand under hand. Feet are held for easier climbing.
- Climb the rope three to five feet with use of the feet as a guide; slowly come back down hand under hand.
- Double ropes: Skin the cat; hold onto two ropes about shoulder height and kick legs and feet over backwards to touch the mat, and then return to starting position.

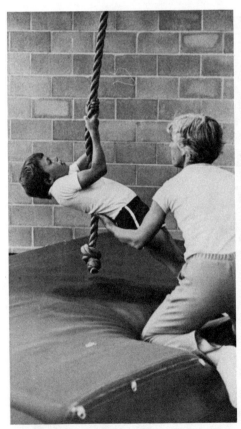

Pulling the body up to a stand from a lying position.

Climbing the rope.

Skin the cat.

BALANCE BEAM

- Squat turn: In a squat position, hands on shoulders, make a half turn on toes. The back should be flat and not rounded.
- Duck walk across the beam: With hands on shoulders, walk in a squat position across the beam, keeping back as flat as possible. Same position as squat turn.

Squat turn.

One-leg balance.

Walking on a higher beam.

- One-leg balance: Balance on one leg, take a step and balance on the other leg.
- Walk on a higher beam with a spotter.

SINGLE BAR
(use chalk for hands)

- Always review chin-ups and pull-ups.
- Pendulum swings forward and back with a tight body and pointed toes. SPOT at hips.
- Pendulum swing same as above but dismount off the back swing, landing in a bent knee position. SPOT at the hips.
- Pendulum swing forward and back with half twists and traveling across the bar, changing grips at the peak of the swing. When spotting at the hips, help the child to turn the body on the peak of the swing.
- From a straight body-hang position, lift legs to 45° and bring them slowly down. Repeat until the legs can go to 90°, and bring them down slowly.

Pendulum swing.

Dismounting off the back swing (right).

Pendulum swing forward and back with half twists (below).

Straight body-hang position, legs lifted to 45° (below right).

Seat drop.

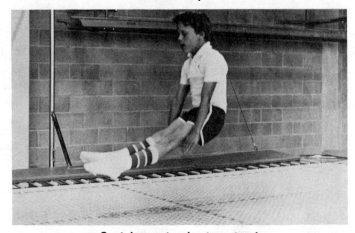

Seat drop, returning to a stand.

TRAMPOLINE

- Seat drop with hands at sides and toes pointed.
- Seat drop, return to a stand with stretched arms overhead.
- Three seat drops consecutively; seat stretch, seat stretch, seat stretch.
- Half turns: Jump and turn half way around, arms overhead (which helps to keep balance) Note: Look over the shoulder in the direction of the turn.
- Seat drop to knee bounce to stand.
- Dog drop, seat drop, and knee bounce: Drop down to a dog bounce and push off to a seat drop. Then push off and tuck knees under a knee bounce, and bounce to a stand.

SAMPLE CHECK-OFF LIST OR CARDS FOR PRESCHOOLERS AT LEVEL II

Name _____

LEVEL II

Hanging Ropes
____ • Pull body up from lying position
____ • Climb rope 3-5 feet
____ • Double ropes; skin the cat

Balance Beam
____ • Squat turn, hands on shoulders
____ • Duck walk
____ • One leg balance
____ • Walk on higher beam

Single Bar
____ • Pendulum swings
____ • Pendulum swing, dismount
____ • Pendulum swing, half twists
____ • Lift legs to 45°-90°

Trampoline
____ • Seat drop, hands at sides
____ • Seat drop to stretched arms
____ • Three seat drops consecutively
____ • Half turns
____ • Seat drop to knee bounce to stand
____ • Dog drop to seat drop to knee bounce to stand

Stunts
____ • Seal walk
____ • Inch worm
____ • V-sit
____ • Tripod
____ • Forward roll
____ • Lead up to cartwheel

PART III
TINY TOTS
Ages 5 - 7

5
THE GYMNASTIC READINESS TEST FOR TINY TOTS

The gymnastic readiness test for tiny tots consists of twenty skills. Each skill is judged on a scale ranging from one to five points, with five being the best score.

The test is worth 100 points (20 skills × 5 points). The child who records a score of 80-100 points is judged to be in a state of very good physical preparedness; 60-79 is considered satisfactory physical preparedness; 40-59 is fair; anything under 40 indicates very poor physical preparedness.

The child can take the test as many times as necessary to improve his/her skills. Meanwhile, the strengths and weaknesses of each child can be determined before he or she starts the gymnastic activities prescribed in Levels I, II, and III.

GYMNASTIC READINESS TEST FOR AGES FIVE, SIX, AND SEVEN

NAME				
DESCRIPTION OF SKILL				
Flex arm hang (strength in arms): The child jumps up on a bar, a rope, or a pair of rings, and holds this position for ten seconds.				
Pull-ups (strength in arms): Hands on a chinning bar with fingers facing out, the child does three pull-ups from a straight body hang.				
Standing broad jump (explosion power of legs): Stand behind a line and jump forward as far as possible without falling back on hands or buttocks. Jump at least three feet.				
Sit-ups (stomach strength): With knees bent and feet held down, do ten sit-ups.				
Straight body push-ups (arm strength): Do three full push-ups, or six half push-ups. (half way to floor and up)				
Forward roll (balance and agility): From a squat position, roll forward in a tuck position to a squat and up to a stand.				
Head to knees (flexibility): Sit with legs straight and try to touch the knees with the nose for two seconds.				
Two arm cartwheel (coordination, flexibility and strength): Execute a side cartwheel hand, hand, foot, foot.				
One arm cartwheel (flexibility, strength, and coordination): Execute a side cartwheel placing only the first hand down on the floor. The other hand is on the hip.				
Headstand from a tripod (neck strength, balance and total body control): Head and hands on the floor with the knees on the elbows. Go into a tight headstand.				
Bridge (flexibility in upper back, upper arms, and shoulders): Lie on back with knees up, feet flat, hands flat with thumbs next to ears, and push with arms up into a bridge.				

GYMNASTIC READINESS TEST FOR AGES FIVE, SIX, AND SEVEN (cont'd.)

NAME				
DESCRIPTION OF SKILL				
Squat up on a bench, beam, or wooden box, at least two feet high (coordination, leg power): From in front of the box, jump, landing on both feet.				
Rope climb five feet (coordination, arm strength): Hand over hand going up, using feet and knees to grip. Come down hand and feet controlled.				
Rope climb five feet (arm strength, coordination): Same as above except use just the arms coming down the rope, hand under hand and legs free from the rope.				
90° angle hang (control, strength in stomach muscles): Hang from a bar or rings, and lift the legs to a 90° angle. Hold five seconds.				
One leg balance on the beam (balance): Lift one leg forward to a 90° angle. Hold five seconds.				
Front pull over on a bar (strength in arms and stomach muscles): Facing the bar, hands and fingers forward wrapped around the bar. Kick feet and legs over the bar and continue around to a support.				
Controlled skin the cat and return (flexibility and strength): This is done between two ropes, a chinning bar or a pair of rings. Pull legs through arms or under bar and remain upside down looking at the knees, and return back around.				
Backward shoulder roll to knees (coordination): Lying on the floor, roll back over one shoulder, moving the head to the side as the legs and feet pass over.				
Backward roll to squat (coordination and arm strength): Same as above except the child will place hands next to ears flat on the floor to push when rolling backwards to feet.				

6
WARM-UP EXERCISES

Start easy, then lengthen each exercise. The first twelve movements deal with getting the body warmed up as well as strengthening the legs, then go right into general stretching and strengthening exercises.

- **Walking:** Swing arms, tummy in, and walk in a large circle.
- **Jogging:** Go right into jogging from walking; swing elbows and jog several times around the circle.
- **Running:** Continue from jogging to running, circling legs like riding a bicycle, and moving elbows back and forth.
- **Repeat #3:** Run the other way around the circle several times.
- **Side gallop:** Without stopping in #4 go right into the side gallop around the circle several times.
- **Repeat #5:** Side gallop the other way around the circle several times.
- **Skipping:** Go right into skipping forward from the side gallop. Try skipping backwards once around.
- **Jog backwards:** Go right into jogging backwards from skipping backwards.
- **Jumping:** Jump forward once around the circle, both feet together; repeat backwards once around the circle. Do ten to fifteen jumps at a time.

- **Hopping:** Alternating feet, go once around the circle, hopping five times on each foot.
- **Jumping jacks:** Place hands on hips and jump to a straddle, then back with feet together. Repeat apart, together, ten times. Add arms together with feet: Slowly jump to a stride with hands over head and then jump back to starting position with hands and arms down at sides and legs together. As the coordination improves, do twenty-five rhythmically.

Jumping jacks.

- **Ankle exercises:** Walk high on balls of feet around in a circle, then change to walking on heels once around the circle. Next walk around the circle on the outside of the feet and then once around the circle on the inside of the feet. Check preschool exercises for a picture of this exercise.

One of the most efficient and effective ways to reduce injury to the muscles, is to stretch properly before and after an activity. When stretching, pull until it is a full stretch but not until it is painful. Stop before it hurts and that will be a strong stretch, hold for 10-15 seconds and relax.

Side stretches.

- **Side stretches (Standing):** With arms stretched over head and legs apart, stretch to the right side, then back up to a stretch forward with a flat back, and then back to starting position. Repeat five times.
- **Back of the legs stretch:** Squat position, hands flat on the floor; raise the buttocks up to stretched legs and back down to a squat. Repeat five times.
- **Hurdle stretch:** With arms stretched over head and legs in a hurdle position on the floor, lean toward the forward foot, grab the ankle and hold for fifteen seconds. Relax. Repeat with other leg. Twice on each leg.
- **Bridges:** Lying on back, knees bent, feet flat on the floor and hands flat next to the ears with fingers pointing toward the shoulders, push the body up, extending arms so that the hands remain under the shoulders and the feet flat to form an arch. Make sure the child does not push from the toes and legs, as this will make him lazy in the arms. If the child is very flexible, try one leg up, making a straight line from the leg to the arms. When doing bridges, assist the child at the upper back, so that he/she can feel the stretch from the arms into the shoulders, and not on the lower back.

Back of the legs stretch.

Hurdle stretch.

Warm-up Exercises

Bridges.

Roll back roll up.

The bridge with one leg up.

Warm-up Exercises

Push-ups.

Bent knee sit-ups.

V-sit hold.

- **Roll back roll up:** Hug knees and roll back to the neck and shoulders, and without stopping, roll up to a sitting position. Doing this several times will stretch the back after the tightening of the muscles from the bridge exercise.
- **Push-ups:** Emphasis on a straight and tight body (tummy in, and squeeze the buttocks). Lower body half-way, bending at the elbows and then return to the starting position. Work up to ten. These are called half push-ups.
- **Bent knee sit-ups:** Lying straight on the back, bring knees and the upper part of the body (chest and head) up at the same time, rest on the buttocks, balance for three seconds and return to prone position. Work up to fifteen sit-ups. (If this type of sit-up is too hard at the beginning, return to the bent-knee sit-up with someone holding feet.)
- **V-sit hold:** After the stomach muscles have been strengthened by performing the bent-knee sit-ups, try this exercise to strengthen the back, thighs, and the abdominals. While balancing on buttocks, arms stretched out, knees bent, keeping the back flat, stretch the legs straight out to form a "V"; hold for three to five seconds, working up to ten. Return to bent-knee and balancing on the buttocks and repeat several times.

With hands on shoulders, walking forward.

7
GYMNASTIC ACTIVITIES

LEVEL I

BALANCE BEAM

This is the same low beam as in the preschool beam activities.

- With hands on shoulders, walk forward, lifting one leg at a time to a 45° angle, toes pointed outward. Eyes should be looking at the end of the beam, never down as it will cause loss of balance. Keep tummy in and hips tight while working the beam (keep hip area in control).
- Same as above only walk backwards, keeping eyes focused on the end of the beam, one step behind the other.
- Walk sidewards slightly on toes, hands on shoulders and eyes straight. Try walking sidewards, crossing feet.
- Squat turn: Squat down with a straight back and stay up on toes and turn 180°. There is only one direction in which the child can turn, otherwise the legs will tangle.

Walking sidewards.

Squat turn.

"V" sit.

One leg squat.

- "V" sit: From a squat position, reach back with the hands to grab the beam and sit down with the legs in a "V" position. Back and legs are straight with toes pointed.
- One leg squat: Arms can be out to the side for balance. Lift one leg to 90° and squat down onto the beam. Quickly grab the beam behind with both hands and go right into a "V" sit. From this position, lie back on the beam to a straight lying position balance. Return to resting on buttocks and knees bent to go into the one leg squat position as shown in picture. Arms come forward as the child rises to a stand with the arms stretched overhead.

TRAMPOLINE

All skills are executed in the center of the trampoline. Traveling around the trampoline bed when executing the skills will cause accidents. Children are taught to keep tight bodies while performing on this apparatus.

- Knee bounce: Bounce on knees with arms swinging up and around until the child can bounce off the knees to a stand. (A knee drop skill is not taught at these beginning levels.)
- Jump three times with arms circling up, out to the sides, and down. As the child jumps up, the arms will go up and out to the sides so that when the child comes down on the trampoline bed, the arms are coming in toward the waist and ready for another jump. If the arms circle around back of child, he/she then loses balance and coordination of the jump. When stopping to gain control of the bounce (or any skill), lower the center of gravity by bending at the knees to almost a squat.

Knee bounce.

Jump.

Seat drop to a stand.

Dog bounce.

- Seat drop to a stand: Keep legs straight and toes pointed upon landing in the seat-drop position, with hands at the sides to maintain perfect balance. Push off with hands to a stretched stand with arms stretched overhead. Arms play a very important part in the safety and balance of trampoline skills.
- Dog bounce: On knees and hands, bounce on the trampoline until the knees and hands at the same time are bouncing off the trampoline. This takes a little practice, as the knees want to bounce and the hands don't. Once coordinated, it is easy.
- Dog bounce to a knee bounce to a stand.

HANGING ROPES
(use chalk on hands)

These are exercises to help teach the child how to climb.

- Jump up and grab the rope with bent arms for five to ten seconds.
- From a sitting position, pull the body up to a stand hand-over-hand with someone holding the feet.
- From a lying position, keeping the body stiff, pull hand-over-hand up to a stand. The feet should be held slightly. If this is very hard, give a little assistance under the hips.

From a lying position, pulling hand-over-hand to a stand.

SINGLE BAR
(use chalk on hands)

- Chin-ups: Fingers are wrapped around the bar, facing the child. If a child can not do a chin-up, refer to chin-downs in the preschool section under Level I. The chin-downs can lead to accomplishing the chin-up.
- Pull-ups: Fingers are wrapped around the bar away from the child. If a child can not do a pull-up, refer to the preschool section under Level I for pull-downs.
- From a straight body hang, hands in a pull-up position, pull feet through hands and under the bar; hook knees on top of the bar and hang free. Spot at the shoulders and hold feet. Return to a straight body hang. Most children can do this by themselves.

| Chin-ups. | Pull-ups. |

Hanging by the knees.

TUMBLING

- Back shoulder roll to knees: From a squat position, roll back over one shoulder keeping hips high enough to plant one knee down on the floor.
- From a squat position, roll back onto shoulders, hugging knees; without stopping, roll back up past the squat position to a stand.
- Tripod (lead up to a headstand): With head on the floor and the hands flat in front of the face, shoulder-width apart, place knees on elbows and balance with a flat back. Do not balance on the very top of the head. Stay closer to the forehead for proper balance.
- With legs in a straddle position, roll forward to a hugging of knees but not to a stand.
- Put second and fourth exercise together for a complete forward roll with arms stretched overhead.

Back shoulder roll to knees.

From squat position to a stand.

Tripod.

From a straddle position (left) to a roll (right).

SWEDISH BOX (low level)

- Progression to vaulting: Practice jumping in place in front of the box (or a bench) with hands on the box, lifting hips high in the air above the box so as to be able to place knees or feet on top of box. Jump three times and place knees on the box. Jump three times and place the feet on the box; then jump off on the other side of the box with a bent-knee landing. Never dismount with stiff legs. Two foot take-off: All vaults are done with a two foot take-off. Step right, left, both feet together for the jump, then place hands on the box and lift hips high, placing feet on box; dismount.

SAMPLE CHECK-OFF LIST FOR TINY TOTS AT LEVEL I

Name _____

LEVEL I

Balance Beam
____ • Walk forward
____ • Walk backwards
____ • Walk sidewards
____ • Squat turn
____ • "V" sit
____ • One leg squat

Trampoline
____ • Knee bounce
____ • Jump and stop for control
____ • Seat drop to a stand
____ • Dog bounce
____ • Dog bounce to knee bounce to a stand

Ropes
____ • Jump and hold 5-10 seconds
____ • Pull to a stand from a sitting position
____ • Pull to a stand from a lying position

Single Bar
____ • Chin-ups
____ • Pull-ups
____ • Knee hang

Tumbling
____ • Back shoulder roll
____ • Tuck position, roll back on shoulders and up to a stand
____ • Tripod (frog stand)
____ • Forward roll to tuck
____ • Forward roll to tuck to a stand and stretch

Swedish Box
____ • Take-off
____ • Jumping in place, hands on box, getting hips high on take-off

LEVEL II

BALANCE BEAM

Use a low beam, six inches off the floor. After the new skills are learned, the child can advance to a beam of about twenty-four inches in height and four inches in width.

- Step-hops the length of the beam: Actually this is a slow skip.
- Step-together-step: Step right, bring left foot up to meet the right foot, step right and repeat to end of beam. Try this, using the left foot first.
- Step right, lift left leg to a 90° angle keeping the back straight and the leg angled slightly out with pointed toes, step left, etc.

Step hops.

Step-together-step (left).

Step, lifting leg to a 90° angle (below left).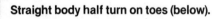

Straight body half turn on toes (below).

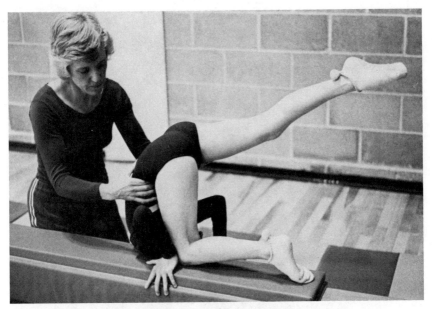

Back shoulder roll on the beam.

- Straight body half turn on toes: The direction in which you will turn is dependent upon which foot is ahead at the start. If the right foot is ahead of the left, then you will turn to the left on the balls of the feet and upon completion of the turn, lower the feet down to the beam. Arms are moving all the time you are turning. Take them up over-head as you turn, and bring them down at the sides upon completion of the turn.
- Back shoulder roll on beam (use a pad for the shoulder): Practice this on the floor first to see which shoulder is preferred. Place on the floor tape that is the width of the beam on the floor. Spotters should help the child at the hips by lifting the hips to help him/her through the roll. If the roll is over the right shoulder, place the head down along the left side of the beam. Hold onto the beam from underneath, elbows close together. Bend the knees and lift hips and legs over the shoulder, placing the right knee on the beam over the right shoulder as close as possible, and start to transfer weight onto the knee, at the same time placing hands on top of the beam. The other leg comes down to the side of the beam and up onto the beam to step up to a stand.
- Routine: "V" sit, swing legs down and behind to a squat position to a stand. Step-hop across the beam to a squat turn, stand, step-together-step to the middle of the beam. Using a straight body turn (½) on toes, do a one-leg squat to a back shoulder roll to a stand.

Jumping and touching the toes in a straddle position.

TRAMPOLINE

For safety, there must be four spotters around the trampoline.

- Jump to a half turn, taking arms over head on the turn.
- Jump and touch toes in a straddle position. Start with touching the knees then ankles and then toes.
- Jump down to a dog drop, then to a seat drop, then push off to a stand.
- Jump to a seat drop, then to a dog drop, and up to a stand.
- Jump to a half turn and without an extra bounce, go right into a seat drop.
- Jump to a seat drop, then to a knee bounce, back to a seat drop, etc. Have a contest to see who can make it to ten bounces.

Up and down climb.

HANGING ROPES
(use chalk for hands)

- Climb the rope three to five feet, and come down hand under hand, controlled. Spot, allowing for slipping.
- Double hanging ropes:
  a. Skin the cat: Place a rope in each hand at shoulder height. Kick legs over the head and touch the floor or mat and return. Spot under the shoulders.
  b. Inverted hang: Same as above except place the legs up the sides of the rope so the child is up-side-down. Spot under the shoulders to avoid slipping.

Skin the cat.

Inverted hang.

SINGLE BAR

- Tight body swing: Swing back and forth, keeping a tight body with no arch; jump off on the back swing to a bent knee landing.
- Review chin-ups and pull-ups, working up to five.
- Penny drop: From a knee hang, the spotter swings the child forward and back. On the count of three on the forward swing, the child releases the legs to a bent knee landing. Spot under the arm so the child does not fall backwards on the landing.

Penny drop.

- Kick legs over the bar to a front support with arms straight and the body tight. From the front support on the bar, roll forward on *thighs* (not on the stomach area), controlled, to a long hang.

TUMBLING

- Back roll: From a squat position, roll backwards, placing hands near ears; push from hands to a straddle position onto feet (head should barely touch floor). Spot, lifting hips.
- Forward roll: From a squat position, lift hips and push from the feet, rolling forward with the head barely touching, to a stand and stretch (tucked forward roll).
- From a frog stand or tripod, hold a balance with knees off elbows and back flat, ready to go into a headstand.
- Headstand: From above point toes and proceed to a tight headstand and back down, controlled, to a squat.
- Back roll to a squat: Spot by lifting the hips so the child can push.
- Headstand to a handstand with a spotter lifting the body by the ankles: at the same time, the child should push extending the arms to the handstand. This teaches the feel of a handstand. From this position, let the child roll out, doing a forward roll to a stand. This combination introduces a handstand forward roll.

Back roll to a straddle position.

Going into a headstand from a tripod position.

Headstand.

Back roll to a squat (above).

Headstand to a handstand (above right).

Forward roll from a handstand (right).

Going into a handstand.

Forward cartwheel.

Forward cartwheel.

- Handstand: Stand, stretching arms over head with one foot in front of the other, with the back leg as the kicking leg. Bending the knee of the front leg, place hands on the floor shoulder-width apart. At the same time, push off with front leg and kick with back leg until the hips are over the head. Toes should be pointed, abdomen tight, squeeze the buttocks, and keep the head down, ears next to the arms. Also try to push out of the shoulders to get a straight, tight body handstand with no arch. Spotter should stand at the side of the child to catch the feet and guide him or her to the proper position.
- Forward cartwheel: Right side as well as left side cartwheel should be taught. Start the same as the handstand. The spotter stands behind the child with arms crossed at the child's waist. As the child kicks over sidewards, the spotter's arms will unfold. Back leg is the kick leg and the front leg is the push-off leg. Hands are placed in line with the feet so that a cartwheel is done in a straight line, hand, hand, foot, foot. End in starting position, arms above head. This is the cartwheel that is executed on the balance beam, not the side cartwheel as taught in Level III under tumbling.

SWEDISH BOX

(this could be a sturdy padded bench or a homemade swedish box as in the picture)

- Hurdle step for the take-off: This is not the same type of hurdle and take-off that a diver uses. This hurdle is low and long before the take-off. Use a small take-off board of about four to six inches of an incline if it is to be homemade. It should be about three feet in length and two feet wide (any gymnasium would have samples to look at). For these skills, a take-off board would not be needed, it just makes it easier for the child to get over the box. Slowly walk toward the box using the hurdle, step right, step left, and with both feet together, jump to a squat on the box, stand and jump off with a bent-knee landing. Spot at the take-off spot to aid the child up on the box.
- Hurdle to a straddle onto the box: From the straddle position on the box, jump to a squat and dismount in a bent-knee landing. Spotter aides the child by standing in front of the box spotting at the shoulders so the child will not fall backwards. Then, the spotter moves back a few steps so the child can dismount.

Jumping over the Swedish box.

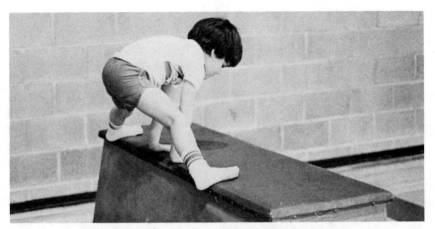

Hurdle to a straddle onto the box.

Dismounting.

Squat vault.

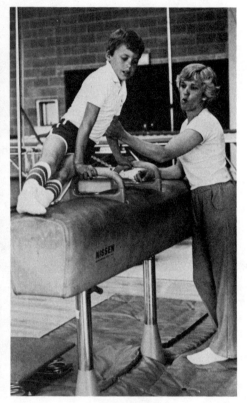

Side vault.

Forward roll on the Swedish box.

- Do two vaults over the box using the hurdle:
  a. Squat vault: Run several steps, then hurdle and jump to a squat: without stopping, take feet through to the other side for a dismount.
  b. Side vault: Run several steps, then hurdle and jump, both legs straight out to the side, over the box, dismounting on the other side. For both (a) and (b), spot at the take-off spot to aid the child up on the box.
- Turn the box around so that the approach is at the end. Run several steps, then hurdle and jump to a squat on the end of the box. Do a forward roll to a stand across the box, and jump off at the other end to a bent-knee dismount. Try dismounting with a half-turn and land in a bent-knee position. Spot the forward roll.

RINGS

- From a straight body hang:
  a. Lift the legs to an "L" (90° angle) position; hold three to five seconds.
  b. Lift the legs to a tuck position to a "skin the cat," bringing knees back over head toward the floor, returning to a long hang. Spot under the shoulders with one hand and guide the body with the other hand.
  c. Lift the legs to a tuck position and insert the feet into the rings; turn the body inside out to make a "bird's nest."

Legs at a 90° angle.

Skin the cat.

Bird's nest.

PARALLEL BARS

All the exercises are done under the bars.

- Swing underneath the bars: Without allowing the feet to touch the floor, travel the length of the bars, swinging from side to side.
- Half twists on one bar: Same as the half twists in Level I on the single bar.
- Hang by the knees and then go into a "skin the cat" exercise. Return the feet back under the bar to the floor.
- Swing side to side sliding hands down one bar; cross over to the other bar and repeat down that bar.
- Creative activity: The child climbs over and under the bars to see how many different positions or exercises can be created.

Swinging underneath the bars.

Half twists on one bar (left).

Hanging by the knees (below left).

Swinging side to side (below).

Creative activity.

Creative activity.

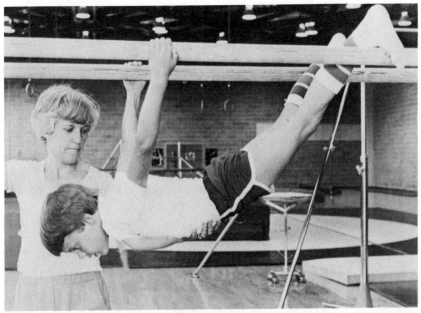

Creative activity.

LEVEL III

BALANCE BEAM

Practice these skills on the low beam before advancing to a medium level beam.

- Inch worm across the beam: This is an exercise for the arms as well as stretching the back of the legs.
- Walk forward the length of the beam on toes, lifting one leg at a time to a 90° angle. Hands can be on shoulders for balance.
- Spin turn: Step left with arms held horizontally to the right. Swing right leg with bent knee around for a half turn, and stop in a lunge position, right leg forward. The turn is done on the ball of the left foot. Try turning on the right foot.
- Walk fast across the beam, keeping the tummy in and the toes pointed outward slightly; arms out to the sides.
- Forward head roll: In a squat position, place the hands about 20" in front of the feet, thumbs on top of the beam and fingers grasping the sides. Bending the elbows, the child lifts the hips and tucks the head, placing the back of the neck on the beam. The top of the head never touches the beam. Keep the body tight, knees to nose (pike position) and the elbows close to the ears. Hands switch from the top of the beam to the bottom of the beam for support while the back of the neck and the back roll down the beam. Finish the roll by planting one foot on the beam and the other foot forward to a stand. The spotter should stand at the side of the beam and guide the hips to line up with the beam. A small one-inch pad can be wrapped around the beam to cushion the back-bone area. This skill should be tried on the floor to get the feel of the roll to a one-leg squat-up. Tape may be placed on the floor to act as a guide.
- Mounts onto the beam: Stand facing the side of the beam with hands on the top; jump to a straight arm support. If using a take-off, the next mount is done at the end of the beam. Place the board close to the beam. From a short run, use a one-foot take-off and leap onto the beam with the other foot. The child should be taught to focus on the spot where the foot is to be placed on the beam. The spotter runs with the child, lending a hand to help guide the take-off. The last mount is a squat onto the beam. Put the take-off board close (one foot) facing the side of the beam. Using a two-foot take-off from a small run, jump to a squat. The spotter stands on the other side of the beam facing the child and anticipates a forward fall.

Inch worm across the beam.

Spin turn.

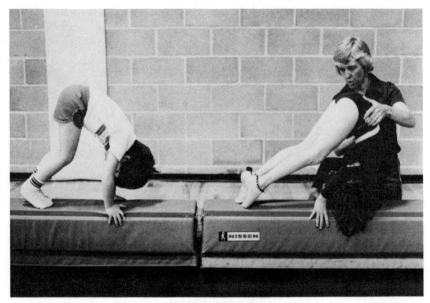

Forward head roll.

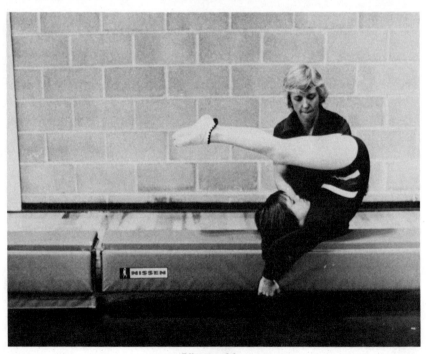

Pike position.

Routine for the beam beginning with a squat mount.

- A simple dismount: From the end or the center of the beam, jump and touch toes in a straddle position and land in a bent-knee position. The spotter stands in front, offering a hand for balance on the dismount.
- Routine for the beam: Mount the beam with a squat mount. From the squat, stand, make a one-quarter turn and step-hop to the end of the beam. Execute a half turn of any style, and step-together-step to the center of the beam. Do a one-leg squat to a "V" sit, lie back on the beam and execute a back shoulder roll to one knee with the other leg straight back. Swing the free leg down and up onto the beam to a stand. Fast walk to the end of the beam and dismount as explained in (G). Spotter should aid the child with the back shoulder roll and the dismount. Stand at the end of the beam in case the child falls back into the beam after the dismount.

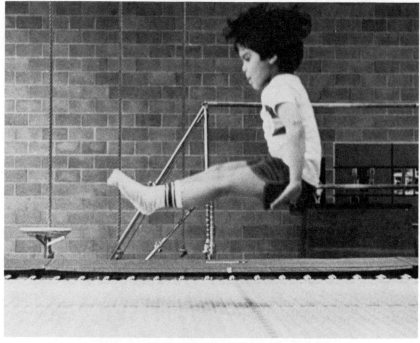

Swivel hips sequence: seat drop.

TRAMPOLINE

This apparatus needs four spotters.

- Review half turn to a seat drop, and seat drop to a half turn. Both of these skills are a lead-up to swivel hips.
- Swivel hips: Seat drop, stretch up to a half turn and back down to a seat drop facing the opposite direction. There are no bounces in between seat drops.
- Jump to a seat drop to a dog bounce to a stand.
- Front drop position from a dog bounce: It is very important that a tight body be taught for the front drop. If a loose or relaxed body should land in a front drop position, it could cause strain on the lower back. The child lies face down on the trampoline, placing the hips at the center of the trampoline. Toes are pointed, with the body stretched and the buttocks squeezed. Now the child is helped into a dog position, bounce from the dog to the stretched front drop position, and back to the dog position. Do this several times until the front drop is tight and the child feels comfortable. A beginner will want to dive forward

Swivel hips sequence: stretch to a half turn.

Swivel hips sequence: seat drop facing the opposite direction.

Front drop position from a dog bounce.

Jumping to a half turn to a knee drop.

towards the springs and this means the body is loose. If a front drop is done from an upright jump, then child could possibly strain the lower back area if the body is not tight upon landing. So always go into the dog position from the upright jump before attempting the front drop. We like to use the dog bounce as a connecting move with developing trampoline skills. A medium level bounce is used to teach the dog drop to the front drop.

- Jump to a seat drop, push to a dog drop, stretch to a front drop and push off to a stand.
- Jump to a half turn to a knee drop. Keep a stiff body upon landing on the knees, with arms out to the sides and the back straight.
- Front drop, half turn to front drop: From a front drop, push off the trampoline with the hands in the direction of the twist. Lift the hips up, keep the head down until the half turn is completed, and stretch for the front drop landing. For the first part of the trick, teach a front drop, then to a half turn to a hands and knees drop (dog bounce). For the second part, the child can do a front drop, dog drop, front drop. (180° turn). In the last part the child is to eliminate the dog drop.

Front drop, half turn to a front drop sequence.

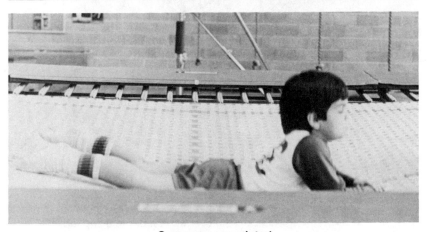

Sequence completed.

HIGH LOWS

These are parallel bars made to look like uneven parallel bars. Spotters stand between the bars for most of the skills.

- Pull-over: Kick over the low bar to a support. In the support position, the thighs are resting on the bar with toes pointed and tummy in, hands in pull-up position.
- From this front support, pike, (bring legs forward under the bar) and thrust the legs backwards to a horizontal position, pushing off the bar to a dismount.
- Facing the low bar, jump and grasp the high bar. In a straddle position, lift legs up and over the low bar to a rest onto the buttocks with a tight body.
- Kick over the high bar: Bend one knee and place that foot on the low bar. This is the "push-off" foot. The leg that is stretched out kicks over the bar at the same time the other leg pushes off the low bar to a front support position on the high bar.

Pull-over sequence: kicking over the low bar to a support position.

Pull-over sequence: Support position with thighs resting on the bar, toes pointed and tummy in (above).

Pull-over sequence: Pike position (upper right).

Pull-over sequence: Thrusting legs backward before pushing off the bar to a dismount (right).

Grasping the high bar (above), then lifting the legs up and over the low bar to a point where they are resting against the buttocks.

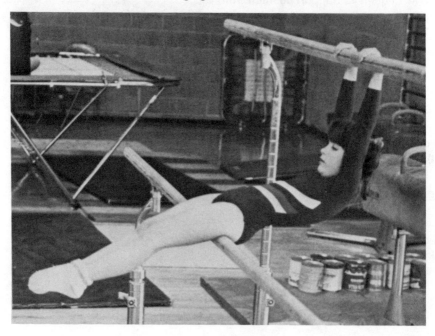

Position for kicking over the high bar.

Kicking over the high bar to a support position.

From the preceding front support position, sliding under the high bar and over the low bar.

- From the front support position, stay as tight as possible and slide under the high bar and over the low bar to the buttocks. Keeping the tight body, turn over to face the low bar and transfer hands to the low bar.
- Cast to a dismount as in the second exercise. This is a "mini" routine but each skill can be taught individually also.
- Back hip circle: From a front support position, keep arms straight, pull legs forward (pike); then cast legs and hips backwards to a horizontal position. Go backwards around the bar by pulling the hips to the bar. As soon as the thighs touch the bar, the child leans back with shoulders and head and proceeds to follow the legs around to a front support. Spotters stand between the bars keeping one hand at the hips and the other helping the legs around.

Turning over to face the low bar and transferring hands to the low bar.

Back hip circle.

SINGLE ROPE ACTIVITY

- Jump rope: There is a lot of creative activity using one six foot rope for each child.
  a. High jump: See who can jump the highest. Have plenty of mats to cushion the fall on the side of the rope where the children land. Work in threes, two hold the rope and one jumps.
  b. Group jump: Arrange your group in a circle with someone in the middle holding the rope. As the rope goes around the circle, each child quickly jumps over it as it reaches him/her.
  c. Make letters and numbers.
  d. Cartwheel over the rope held 10-18 inches high by two children. Rope should be held higher as the cartwheel improves.
  e. Jump to music with the rope.
  f. Lay the rope on the floor in a circle or a straight line and create your own series of movements in and out or around.
  g. Put two ropes parallel to each other on the floor, six to twelve inches apart, and create a series of movements.
  h. Tug of war with partner.

HANGING ROPES
(use chalk)

- Climb ten feet and transfer to the next rope. First transfer the hands to a bent arm position; then transfer the feet and wrap the feet and legs around the rope. Come down controlled. Spot under the two ropes by holding them steady.
- Climb fifteen feet and come down slowly, controlled, with no sliding. Spot the same as in first exercise.
- Climb ten feet and come down controlled, using arms only and legs straight out and away from the rope. Spot the same as in first exercise.
- With two hanging ropes, one in each hand, jump and hold body in a bent arm position for 30 seconds. No spotting needed. Feet are off the floor.
- Swing on the rope and jump off at the end of the back swing. Move backwards as far as possible and jump up on the rope to swing forward to dismount, or jump off at the end of the swing. It can be set up so that the child could jump over an obstacle such as a box, bench, or a stick, raised 20 inches off the floor, or even jump into a held hoop.
- Swing on two ropes, doing the same skills as in above. Swing with two ropes and try landing on top of a bench.

After climbing ten feet up one rope, transferring to the next rope.

Coming down the ropes using the arms only, with legs straight out.

TUMBLING

- Back roll: Roll back onto the shoulders in a tuck position and place hands next to ears as in the bridge. Push with hands and arms to a pike position (legs straight). Spot, lifting the hips.
- Back roll to a walk out: Same as above except only one foot lands in a tuck position and the other leg is extended.
- Handstand to a forward roll: Kick to a handstand with a spotter. Check handstand in Level II under Tumbling. To go into a forward roll from the handstand, extend out of the shoulders by pushing the handstand to a full extension, enough to overbalance; then tuck the head, rolling down the back in a pike or tuck position. Squat up to a stand. Do a handstand forward roll without a spotter.
- Side cartwheel: This time the cartwheel is spread out to an even rhythmical hand, hand, foot, foot. The side cartwheel starts differently from the forward cartwheel in that, the arms are spread further apart (legs and arms are like spokes in a wheel). Draw a line. The left side faces the line, and the arms are stretched overhead. The left knee is in a lunge position for the push-off foot, and the right leg is the kick leg. Push and kick over in a straight line, and land with the left side facing the line again. Do two or three in a row and try several to the right also. If spotting is needed, refer to Forward Cartwheel in Level II under Tumbling.

Back roll.

Completing the back roll.

Back roll to a walk out.

Side cartwheel.

One-arm cartwheel.

Round-off.   **Completing the round-off.**

- One-arm cartwheel: Support the body on one hand doing the side cart-wheel. Repeat above going to the left, using the left hand as the first hand down. Put the right hand on the right hip and kick. Try it on the right hand also.
- Round-off: The first half of the round-off is the forward cartwheel. When the body is in the handstand position halfway through the cart-wheel, both legs come together and snap down, landing in a bent-knee position. To practice the snap down, kick into a handstand, lower the body, bending at the elbows about two inches, and push-off from the floor, pushing out of the shoulders and snapping the feet down to the floor.
- Tumbling run: Handstand forward roll, forward cartwheel, round-off, back roll to a straddle, back straddle roll walk-out, and stretch straight up to a stand.

RINGS
(use chalk)

- Straight body pull-up: As many as possible. If a pull-up can not be done, start with "pull-downs," as in Bars in Level I of this chapter.
- Pendulum swing: Just the body moves back and forth as the rings are still. Swing the legs forward lifting the legs to a pike-like position, then swing back to a slightly arched position. This is good for the shoulders.
- Review "skin the cat" and the "bird's nest" hang from Level II in this chapter.
- Inverted hang: From a straight body hang, lift the legs to a pike position and shoot legs straight up to an inverted position. Return to a pike position, then to a long hang. The spotter for these last three exercises should stand next to the child and put a hand under the child's back and shoulders.

Straight body pull-up.

Pendulum swing.

Pendulum swing.

Inverted hang.

Inverted hang.

SWEDISH BOX

Depending on the size of the child and his or her ability, the box could be raised accordingly and a take-off board added, the vaulting becomes complete (the board can be padded). Spotter stands between the take-off board and the box.

- Squat vault
- Side vault
- Try a headstand to a forward roll on top of the box. No board needed. This should be done on the lower box first.
- Tug of war: Stand on top of the box with a partner and have a tug of war with a small rope (try low level first).

Squat vault.

BALANCE BEAM FOR FUN

(at medium height)

- Round-off dismount: The child stands about three feet from the end of the beam. Place hands on the edge of the beam and kick the legs into a round-off to dismount onto the floor. Check "tumbling" for the round-off in this level. The spotter supports the child's upper arms from behind, moving right along with the child to prevent a fall backwards from the dismount. It's important that the spotter asks the child which way the cartwheel is to be executed, to the right or to the left, or the spotter will be kicked. Also the spotter will know on which side of the beam to stand.
- Straddle mount: Using a two-foot take-off from the take-off board, straddle onto the beam with most of the weight on the hands and then do a quarter turn with all the weight on the hands, freeing the feet from the beam, to a "V" sit.

Round-off dismount.

Straddle mount.

Straddle half turn.

• Straddle half turn: From a "V" sit, lower legs and lean on the beam with your hands in front of you, lifting the hips off the beam. Start the half turn, legs free from the beam and swinging legs level to the opposite direction. Spot from behind the child, guiding the 180° turn at the waist.

Straddle half turn.

Wolf mount.

- Wolf mount: Mount the beam from a two-foot take-off with one foot in a squat position and the other leg stretched out to the side. Spotter is facing the child, reaching for the shoulders.
- Wolf mount half turn: Balancing on the squatted foot, swing the stretched leg and the arms towards the squatted foot halfway around, facing opposite direction. If the child is flexible enough, see if he/she can slide right into a forward split (one leg forward and one leg back) or a side split (straddle split). Spotter stands behind as the child's balance might tend to go backward. It is easier for the child to jump forward than to fall off backwards.

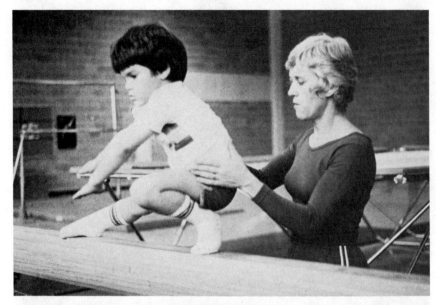

Wolf mount half turn.

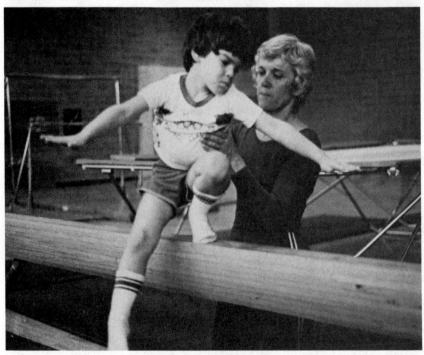

Wolf mount half turn.

LOW BEAM

- Push-ups on the beam.
- Wheelbarrow walk with a partner across the beam.
- Use a hoop like a jump rope as well as a rope.
- Do a forward cartwheel on the beam: Try to place the first foot down on the beam very close to the hands. Do not spread the cartwheel out. Both hands are placed on the beam at the same time. Spot from behind, the same as in tumbling (180° turn).

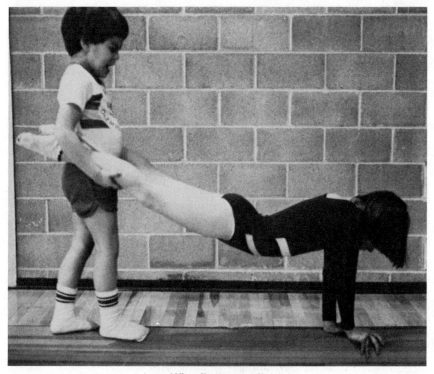

Wheelbarrow walk.

SAMPLE CHECK-OFF LIST FOR TINY TOTS AT LEVEL III

Name _____

LEVEL III
Balance Beam
_____ • Inch worm across beam
_____ • Lift leg 90°
_____ • Spin turn
_____ • Walk fast
_____ • Forward head roll
_____ • Mounts
_____ • Dismount
_____ • Routine

Trampoline
_____ • Half turn to seat drop
_____ • Swivel hips
_____ • Seat drop to dog drop to stand
_____ • Front drop position
_____ • Seat drop, dog drop, to front drop to stand
_____ • Half turn to knee drop
_____ • Dog drop to front drop, half turn in dog position to another front drop

High-Lows
_____ • Pull over
_____ • Front support, cast to dismount
_____ • Grab high bar, lift legs over low bar in straddle position
_____ • Kick over high bar
_____ • Slide down to low bar
_____ • Cast to dismount like second exercise
_____ • Back hip circle

Single Rope Activities
_____ • 6-8 foot length rope: High jump, group jump, make numbers and letters, cartwheel over the rope, tug of war and create many more

Hanging Ropes
_____ • Climb to 10 feet, transfer to next rope and down
_____ • Climb 15 feet, and down slowly
_____ • Climb 10 feet, and come down slowly
_____ • Jump and hang 30 seconds on two ropes
_____ • Swing with rope
_____ • Swing with two ropes

Gymnastic Activities

Tumbling
____ • Back roll
____ • Back roll to walkout
____ • Handstand to forward roll
____ • Side cartwheel
____ • One arm cartwheel
____ • Round-off
____ • Tumbling run

Rings
____ • Pull-up
____ • Pendulum swing
____ • Review "skin the cat" and "nest hang"
____ • Inverted hang

Swedish Box
Raise box to next level depending on child
____ • Squat vault
____ • Side vault
____ • Headstand to forward roll
____ • Tug of war on low box first before the next level

Balance Beam for Fun
(medium height beam)
____ • Dismount
____ • Straddle mount
____ • Straddle half turn
____ • Wolf mount
____ • Wolf mount with half turn
    On low beam
    ____ • Push-ups
    ____ • Wheelbarrow walk
    ____ • Hoop and rope jumping on beam
    ____ • Forward cartwheel on beam

PART IV
STUNTS
AND FUN
FOR ALL

8
STUNTS FOR AGES THREE THROUGH SEVEN

SINGLE STUNTS

Log roll: Child lies on the mat with arms stretched overhead, and twists hips and shoulders equally as he/she rolls down the mat ten feet or so. Repeat rolling the other way. The tighter the body, the straighter the roll.

Lame dog walk: In a squat position, place hands on the floor in front. Lean forward and extend one leg backwards, moving on three limbs.

Elephant walk: With legs in a straddle position, bend at the waist and drag the hands along the floor from side to side, walking forward. Hands are the elephants' trunk.

Crab walk forward and backward: Sit on the floor with the hands behind and the knees bent in front. Raise hips and walk forward twenty feet; then walk backwards twenty feet.

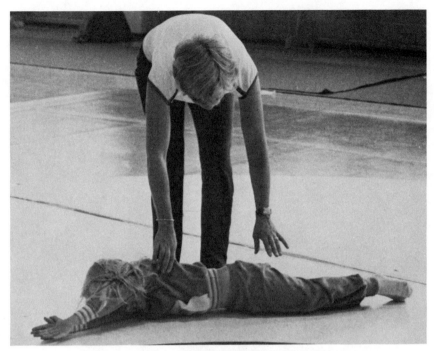

Log roll.

Lame dog walk.

Elephant walk.

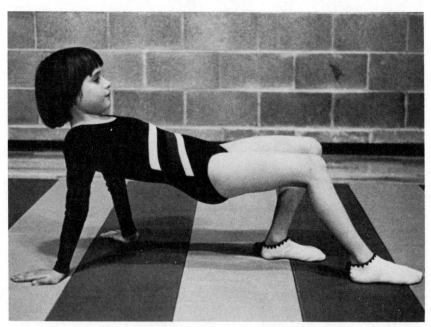

Crab walk forward and backward.

Seal walk: In a push-up position, extend ankles with the weight on top of toes. Walk with hands, dragging legs and toes, trying not to let the back sag.

Kangaroo hop: From a squat position, jump straight up into the air, extending arms overhead; return to a squat position.

Seal walk.

Kangaroo hop.

Duck walk: From a squat position, fold hands under the arms and start walking, lifting legs to the side and forward, leaning from side to side.

Dog walk: In a squat position, reach out and place hands on the floor and walk forward, imitating a dog. Walk sidewards and backwards as well as forward.

Rabbit hop: In a squat position, place hands flat on the floor in front. Reach out with the hands, then bring the feet up towards the hands, transferring the weight from the hands to the feet to keep the body moving forward.

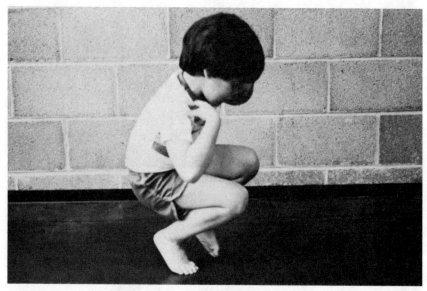

Duck walk.

Rabbit hop.

Inch worm.

Shoulder rest.

Inch worm: From a push-up position, start the feet inching up towards the hands, keeping the legs very straight. When the legs can't go any further forward without bending the knees, then start inching the hands forward to the push-up position.

Shoulder rest: (Inverted balance) Lie on the floor. Lift the legs up to an inverted position with the hands holding the hips up. Roll back down to a lying position. Try this without the hands holding the hips. Hands would be flat on the floor.

Jump and slap heels.

Jump and slap heels: From a standing position with hands at sides, jump and slap heels and return to standing position.

Turk stand.

"V" sit.

Tripod.

Turk stand: From a standing position with arms and legs crossed, place weight on the outer edges of the feet. Slowly lower the body to the floor. To get up, place weight over the feet and rise to original position.

"V" sit: Sitting on the floor and balancing on the buttocks, try to place the legs straight out at a 45° angle with the hands out to the sides.

Tripod: Place the head on the floor and hands flat in front of the face, shoulder width apart, place the knees on the elbows and balance. Head and hands form a triangle.

Coffee grinder.

Tip-up.

Coffee grinder: Place on hand flat on the floor, with the rest of the body extended out; start walking the legs around in a circle. After circling once, lean on the other hand.

Tip-up: In a squat position, place hands shoulder width apart flat on the floor. Put the knees on the elbows, with the head lowered at the same time, balancing on the hands. The head is about three inches from the floor.

DOUBLE STUNTS (with partner)

Wheelbarrow: One child is the wheelbarrow, and one child is the lifter. They should be equal in size. The wheelbarrow is in a push-up position, and the lifter stands between the legs and lifts at the knees. After twenty or thirty feet, the children change positions.

Wheelbarrow.

Double rocker.

Double forward roll.

Double rocker: Both children face each other and sit on each other's feet. Place hands on shoulders and rock back and forth, pulling at the shoulders, and lifting with the feet.

Double forward roll: Base: Lie on the mat with the legs up in a pike position. Grab the ankles of the top person. Top: Stand behind the base's shoulders and reach forward to grasp the ankles of the base. The top begins the roll by leaning forward to place base's feet on the floor and at the same time pushes off the mat pulling the base forward. Now the top becomes the base and the base becomes the top. Roll ten feet.

Leap frog: The base squats down to let the top run and jump from both feet over the base's back, placing hands on the base's back to push off.

Chinese get-up: Partners sit back-to-back with locked elbows, knees bent and feet flat on the floor. Working evenly together, they are to push against each other with their backs and at the same time push on the floor with their feet, rising to a standing position.

Wring the dishcloth: Partners face each other, join hands and turn under the raised arms, ending up back to back. Continue in the same direction, raising the other pair of arms; without releasing hands, turn back around facing each other.

Leap frog.

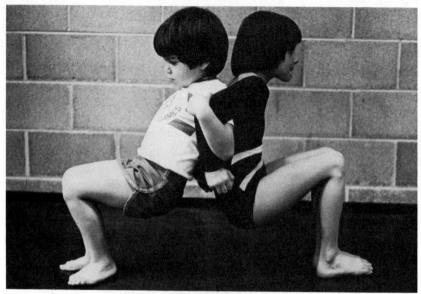

Chinese get-up.

Wring the dishcloth.

9
DEVELOPING HAND-EYE AND BODY COORDINATION USING HAND APPARATUS

HOOPS

Hoops are as much fun for the instructor as they are for the children. The parent or instructor can use them as a tool along with some gymnastic activities, or the child can use them individually.

TYPES OF HOOP ACTIVITIES

- Throw or hit a balloon through a held hoop and run to the other side before the balloon drops to the floor.
- Pick up the hoop with the toes.

- Crawl through one or many hoops on the balance beam, doing a dog walk or a duck walk.
- The child swings on a rope and jumps into a held hoop.
- Use a hoop like a jump rope.
- Jump from a trampolet or a take-off board into a hoop onto a mat.
- Walk on the beam, stepping over the hoop with each step.
- Walk through one or more hoops on the beam without falling off.
- See if the child can keep the hoop circling around the hips.
- Jump into a held hoop from a bench, etc.
- With a spotter protecting the neck, do a forward roll from a squat by reaching across the hoop and roll.

Throwing a balloon through the hoop.

Crawling through hoops.

Swinging on a rope and jumping into a held hoop.

Jumping from a take-off board into a hoop on the mat.

Stepping over the hoop with each step.

Walking through hoops.

Jumping into a held hoop.

Forward roll through a hoop.

Throw and catch with a partner.

BALLOONS

Balloons are used as a progression to ball handling. For example, batting the balloon up in the air with the hands and catching it gives the child time to coordinate his catch.

TYPES OF ACTIVITIES

- Hit the balloon with the hands ten times up into the air without it touching the floor once.
- Throw and catch with a partner.
- Throw the balloon through a hoop and run to the other side to catch it before it hits the floor.
- Try hitting the balloon off a knee or head and catch it before it hits the floor.
- Three or four children in a circle try to keep the balloon in the air before it hits the floor. Use the left hand as well as the right hand.
- Set up a circle of very large tin cans with open end down. Carry two or three balloons and walk from can to can without falling or dropping a balloon.

Hitting the balloon ten times up into the air.

Walking on a circle of cans while carrying two balloons.

WANDS

Wands are 18'' dowels cut from a 36'' dowel which can be purchased at a lumber company. We use them mostly for exercising with the three and four year olds. For a group of children, we place the wands on the floor a couple of feet apart in a big circle so they can jog in and out and leap over them.

TYPES OF INDIVIDUAL ACTIVITIES

- Jump and/or hop over the wand forwards and backwards.
- Jump over and back sidewards.
- Hop over and back sidewards.
- Pick up the wand with the toes.
- Standing, stretch right, left, and forward, with wand overhead.
- Standing or sitting, twist the upper body to the right and left.

Jogging in and out between wands placed on the floor in a big circle.

Stretching to the right and left with wands held overhead.

Stretching forward.

Twisting the upper body to the right and left.

(a). Roll back, roll up.

(b). Moving the wand from under the knees to a position over on top of the knees.

(c). Stretching, with legs in the straddle position.

Stepping over a wand while on the beam.

- Sitting on the floor:
  a. Roll back, roll up with the wand under the knees. Tight tuck roll.
  b. With the wand under the knees and resting on the buttocks, move the wand from under the knees to over on top of the knees.
  c. Legs in straddle position, stretch right, left, and center with the wand.
- Step over a held wand (6-10 inches) while walking the beam.
- Stick horse: Place the wand between the legs and gallop around the area pretending it is a horse.

NERF BALLS

Nerf balls are made from a spongy substance. It is safe to play with indoors, and because of its lightness, it can't be thrown too far. When learning to throw a ball, the children are taught to use both the right and left hands. One disadvantage of this ball is that you cannot bounce it; but we feel there are plenty of skills to be taught without bouncing a ball.

Throwing the ball through a hoop.

TYPES OF ACTIVITIES

- Throw the ball at a target, using the underhand and the overhand throw. Try throwing the ball through a held hoop.
- Jump over the ball.
- Dribble the ball with the feet.
- Throw and catch to themselves.
- Do a rabbit hop and a kangaroo hop over several balls.
- Crab walk forward and backward and carry the ball on the stomach area.
- Crab walk forward and dribble the ball with the feet.
- Balance on the buttocks with legs up; roll the ball under the legs and around back behind, making a complete circle around the body. Roll the ball in the other direction.

Dribbling with the feet.

Throwing and catching to themselves.

Crab walk with the ball on the stomach.

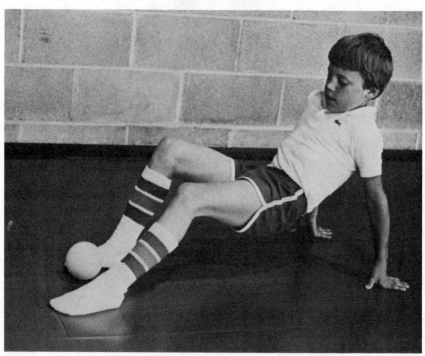

Crab walk forward, dribbling the ball with the feet.

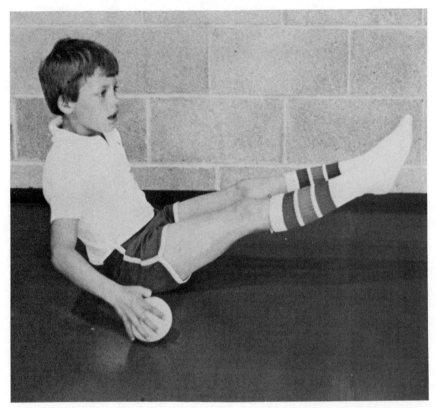

Rolling the ball under the legs and around the back, making a complete circle around the body.

THE AUTHOR

Dancy Kelsey Noble graduated from Springfield College and later received her masters degree from St. Lawrence University. For the last twenty years, she has taught physical education to students of all ages, including college students. During that time she also judged and coached gymnastics in the high schools and set up pilot programs for the very young. She has been certified as an instructor as well as a National Certifier by the United States Gymnastic Safety Association. She directs a gymnastic program for boys and girls ages three through fourteen.